HISTORY'S MOST INFLUENTIAL INVENTORS

FROM THE Late 1900s TO THE 2000s

Frederick Sanger to Sergey Brin

EDITED BY ROBERT CURLEY

Britannica Educational Publishing

IN ASSOCIATION WITH

ROSEN EDUCATIONAL SERVICES

Published in 2025 by Britannica Educational Publishing
(a trademark of Encyclopædia Britannica, Inc.)
in association with Rosen Educational Services, LLC
2544 Clinton Street, Buffalo, NY 14224.

Distributed exclusively by Rosen Educational Services.
For a listing of additional Britannica Educational Publishing titles, call toll free (800) 237-9932.

First Edition

Britannica Educational Publishing
Michael I. Levy: Executive Editor
Marilyn L. Barton: Senior Coordinator, Production Control
Steven Bosco: Director, Editorial Technologies
Lisa S. Braucher: Senior Producer and Data Editor
Yvette Charboneau: Senior Copy Editor
Kathy Nakamura: Manager, Media Acquisition
Robert Curley: Manager, Science and Technology

Editor: Greg Roza
Book design: Michael Flynn

Photo credits: Cover https://commons.wikimedia.org/wiki/File:Sir_Tim_Berners-Lee_(cropped).jpg; p. 41 Featureflash Photo Agency/Shutterstock.com; p. 51 drserg/Shutterstock.com.

Cataloging-in-Publication Data

Names: Curley, Robert, 1955-.
Title: From the late 1900s to the 2000s: Frederick Sanger to Sergey Brin / edited by Robert Curley.
Description: New York : Britannica Educational Publishing, in Association with Rosen Educational Services, 2025. | Series: History's most influential inventors | Includes glossary and index.
Identifiers: ISBN 9781641901024 (library bound) | ISBN 9781641901017 (pbk) | ISBN 9781641901031 (ebook)
Subjects: LCSH: Inventors--Biography. | Inventions--History.
Classification: LCC T39.F766 2025 | DDC 609.2'2--dc23

Manufactured in the United States of America

CPSIA Compliance Information: Batch #CSBRIT25. For further information contact Rosen Publishing at 1-800-237-9932.

CONTENTS

Introduction

"To invent, I draw upon my knowledge, intuition, creativity, experience, common sense, perseverance, flexibility, and hard work."
—Stephanie Kwolek (1923–2014)

Life has been transformed over the years through the efforts of the men and women who had the brilliance, diligence, and creativity to come up with new and better ways of doing things. This book focuses on the inventions of people who lived from the late 1900s to the 2000s. As detailed throughout these pages, their inventions spawned many more inventions, speeding up the pace of progress even further.

The speed of invention today is so rapid that the world can literally change during the course of one individual's lifetime. Someone who was born in the early part of the 20th century will have witnessed the invention of the television, computer, internet, microwave oven, helicopter, penicillin, and dozens of other innovations that have transformed the way in which people live. Looking ahead into the next century, new therapies might be developed that could reprogram human DNA, changing the course of an individual's medical history before he or she is even born. Many inventions have clearly improved life by keeping people healthier, helping them to communicate and work more efficiently, and allowing them to travel farther.

Inventors have had a knack for recognizing a need or problem in society and then discovering a way to fill that need or solve that problem. What ultimately fueled the spark of discovery and led inventors to their "eureka" moment was unique to each person. For example, when

Steve Wozniak, inventor of the Apple II computer, was 11 years old, he built a computer so that he could play tic-tac-toe.

Some of the most groundbreaking and world-changing inventions were not always recognized as such when they were introduced to the public. In 1968, the audience attending a computer conference at the San Francisco Civic Auditorium likely didn't know what to make of Douglas Engelbart's invention—a small wooden box with a button that moved a cursor on an attached machine. His "mouse," so named for its tail-like cable, now enables virtually every home and business computer user to navigate around their computer screens.

Many of the inventors in this book saw great success during their lifetimes. Money was just one of the benefits awarded. Inventors also earned fame, recognition, and a place in history. Some received what is thought to be the highest honor—the Nobel Prize. English biochemist Frederick Sanger was awarded the Nobel Prize in Chemistry twice: once in 1958 and again in 1980 (shared with Paul Berg and Walter Gilbert) for his pioneering work unraveling the mysteries of DNA.

So many inventors have made important contributions in this time period that to mention them all here would far exceed the space limitations of this book. The figures who have been included are among the greatest and most prolific inventors of all time. They were selected because their inventions have altered the course of people's lives and have left an indelible stamp on human history.

FREDERICK SANGER

(b. Aug. 13, 1918, Rendcombe, Gloucestershire, Eng.—d. Nov. 19, 2013, Cambridge)

English biochemist Frederick Sanger was twice the recipient of the Nobel Prize for Chemistry. He was awarded the prize in 1958 for his determination of the structure of the insulin molecule. He shared the prize (with Paul Berg and Walter Gilbert) in 1980 for his determination of base sequences in nucleic acids. Sanger was only the fourth two-time recipient of the Nobel Prize.

Education

Sanger was the middle child of Frederick Sanger, a medical practitioner, and Cicely Crewsdon Sanger, the daughter of a wealthy cotton manufacturer. The family expected him to follow in his father's footsteps and become a medical doctor. After much thought, he decided to become a scientist. In 1936 Sanger entered St. John's College, Cambridge. He initially concentrated on chemistry and physics, but he was later attracted to the new field of biochemistry. He received a bachelor's degree in 1939 and stayed at Cambridge an additional year to take an advanced course in biochemistry. He and Joan Howe married in 1940 and subsequently had three children.

Because of his Quaker upbringing, Sanger was a conscientious objector and was assigned as an orderly to a hospital near Bristol when World War II began. He soon decided to visit Cambridge to see if he could enter the doctoral program in biochemistry. Several researchers there were interested in having a student, especially one who did not need money. He studied lysine metabolism with biochemist Albert Neuberger. They also had a project in support of the war effort, analyzing nitrogen from potatoes. Sanger received a doctorate in 1943.

INSULIN RESEARCH

Biochemist Albert C. Chibnall and his protein research group moved from Imperial College in London to the safer wartime environment of the biochemistry department at Cambridge. Two schools of thought existed among protein researchers at the time. One group thought proteins were complex mixtures that would not readily lend themselves to chemical analysis. Chibnall was in the other group, which considered a given protein to be a distinct chemical compound.

Chibnall was studying insulin when Sanger joined the group. At Chibnall's suggestion, Sanger set out to identify and quantify the free-amino groups of insulin. Sanger developed a method using dinitrofluorobenzene to produce yellow-colored derivatives of amino groups. Information about a new separation technique, partition chromatography, had recently been published. In a pattern that typified Sanger's career, he immediately recognized the utility of the new technique in separating the hydrolysis products of the treated protein. He identified two terminal amino groups for insulin, phenylalanine and glycine, suggesting that insulin is composed of two types of chains. Working with his first graduate student, Rodney Porter, Sanger used the method to study the amino terminal groups of several other proteins. (Porter later shared the 1972 Nobel Prize for Physiology or Medicine for his work in determining the chemical structure of antibodies.)

On the assumption that insulin chains are held together by disulphide linkages, Sanger oxidized the chains and separated two fractions. One fraction had phenylalanine at its amino terminus; the other had glycine. Whereas complete acid hydrolysis degraded insulin to its constituent amino acids, partial acid hydrolysis generated insulin peptides composed of several amino acids. Using another recently introduced technique, paper chromatography, Sanger was able to sequence the amino-terminal peptides of each chain, demonstrating for the first time that a protein has a specific sequence at a specific site. A combination of partial acid hydrolysis and enzymatic hydrolysis allowed Sanger and the Austrian biochemist Hans Tuppy to determine the complete sequence of amino acids in the phenylalanine chain of insulin. Similarly, Sanger and the Australian biochemist E.O.P. Thompson determined the sequence of the glycine chain.

Two problems remained: the distribution of the amide groups and the location of the disulphide linkages. With the completion of those two puzzles in 1954, Sanger had deduced the structure of insulin. For being the first person to sequence a protein, Sanger was awarded the 1958 Nobel Prize for Chemistry.

Sanger and his coworkers continued their studies of insulin, sequencing insulin from several other species and comparing the results. Utilizing newly introduced radiolabeling techniques, Sanger mapped the amino acid sequences of the active centers from several enzymes. One of these studies was conducted with another graduate student, Argentine-born immunologist César Milstein. (Milstein later shared the 1984 Nobel Prize for Physiology or Medicine for discovering the principle for the production of monoclonal antibodies.)

RNA Research

In 1962 the Medical Research Council opened its new laboratory of molecular biology in Cambridge. The Austrian-born British biochemist Max Perutz, British biochemist John Kendrew, and British biophysicist Francis Crick moved to the new laboratory. Sanger joined them as head of the protein division. It was a banner year for the group, as Perutz and Kendrew shared the 1962 Nobel Prize for Chemistry and Crick shared the 1962 Nobel Prize for Physiology or Medicine with the American geneticist James D. Watson and the New Zealand-born British biophysicist Maurice Wilkins for the discovery of DNA (deoxyribonucleic acid).

Sanger's interaction with nucleic acid groups at the new laboratory led to his pursuing studies on ribonucleic acid (RNA). RNA molecules are much larger than proteins, so obtaining molecules small enough for technique development was difficult. The American biochemist Robert W. Holley and his coworkers were the first to sequence RNA when they sequenced alanine-transfer RNA. They used partial hydrolysis methods somewhat like those Sanger had used for insulin. Unlike other RNA types, transfer RNAs have many unusual nucleotides. This partial hydrolysis method would not work well with other RNA molecules, which contain only four types of nucleotides, so a new strategy was needed.

The goal of Sanger's lab was to sequence a messenger RNA and determine the genetic code, thereby solving the puzzle of how groups of nucleotides code for amino acids. Working with British biochemists George G. Brownlee and Bart G. Barrell, Sanger developed a two-dimensional electrophoresis method for sequencing RNA. By the time the sequence methods were worked out, the code had been broken by other researchers, mainly the American biochemist Marshall Nirenberg and the Indian-born American biochemist Har Gobind Khorana, using in vitro protein synthesis techniques. The RNA sequence work of Sanger's group did confirm the genetic code.

DNA Research

By the early 1970s, Sanger was interested in deoxyribonucleic acid (DNA). DNA sequence studies had not developed because of the immense size of DNA molecules and the lack of suitable enzymes to cleave DNA into smaller pieces. Building on the enzyme copying approach used by the Swiss chemist Charles Weissmann in his studies on bacteriophage RNA, Sanger began using the enzyme DNA polymerase to make new strands of DNA from single-strand templates, introducing radioactive nucleotides into the new DNA. DNA polymerase requires a primer that can bind to a known region of the template strand. Early success was limited by the lack of suitable primers. Sanger and British colleague Alan R. Coulson developed the "plus and minus" method for rapid DNA sequencing. It represented a radical departure from earlier methods in that it did not utilize partial hydrolysis. Instead, it generated a series of DNA molecules of varying lengths that could be separated by using polyacrylamide gel electrophoresis. For both plus and minus systems, DNA was synthesized from templates to generate random sets of DNA molecules from very short to very long. When both plus and minus sets were separated on the same gel, the sequence could be read from either system, one confirming the other. In 1977 Sanger's group used this system to deduce most of the DNA sequence of bacteriophage ΦX174. It was the first complete genome to be sequenced.

A few problems remained with the plus and minus system. Sanger, Coulson, and British colleague Steve Nicklen developed a similar procedure using dideoxynucleotide chain-terminating inhibitors. DNA was synthesized until an inhibitor molecule was incorporated into the growing DNA chain. Using four reactions, each with a different inhibitor, sets of DNA fragments were generated ending in every nucleotide. For example, in the A reaction, a series of DNA fragments ending in A (adenine) was generated. In the C reaction, a series of DNA fragments ending in C (cytosine) was generated, and so on for G (guanine) and T (thymine). When the four reactions were separated side by side on a gel and an autoradiograph developed, the sequence was read from the film. Sanger and his coworkers used the dideoxy method to sequence human mitochondrial DNA, the first human gene to be sequenced. For his contributions to DNA sequencing methods, Sanger shared the 1980 Nobel Prize for Chemistry. He retired in 1983.

Additional Honors

Sanger's additional honors included election as a fellow of the Royal Society (1954), being named a Commander of the Order of the British Empire (1963), the Royal Society's Royal Medal (1969), the Royal Society's Copley Medal (1977), election to the Order of the Companions of Honor (1981), and the Order of Merit (1986). In 1992 the Wellcome Trust and the British Medical Research Council established a genome research center, honoring Sanger by naming it the Wellcome Trust Sanger Institute.

TOM KILBURN

(b. Aug. 11, 1921, Dewsbury, Yorkshire, Eng.—d. Jan. 17, 2001, Manchester)

Tom Kilburn was an English engineer and coinventor of the first working computer memory. He also designed and built the first stored-program computer and led a team that produced a succession of pioneering computers over the next 25 years.

In 1942 Kilburn graduated from the University of Cambridge with a degree in mathematics. He immediately converted, however, to electronics research when he was recruited to join Frederic Williams's wartime radar group at the Telecommunications Research Establishment (TRE). In December 1946 Williams left TRE to become a professor at the University of Manchester, and Kilburn accompanied him in order to help develop an electronic storage system for electronic computers. They devised a storage device—later known as the Williams tube—based on cathode-ray tubes. A working model was completed late in 1947, and by June 1948 they had incorporated it in a small electronic computer that they built to prove the device's effectiveness. The computer was called the Small Scale Experimental Machine (SSEM) or just "Baby." It was the world's first working stored-program computer, and the Williams tube became one of the two standard methods of storage used by computers worldwide until the advent of magnetic-core storage in the mid-1950s. By April 1949 the SSEM had developed into a full-sized machine, and by October 1949 secondary storage had been added (using a magnetic drum). This machine, the Manchester Mark I, was the prototype for the Ferranti Mark I, manufactured by Ferranti, Ltd.

From 1951 Kilburn formally led the computer group within Williams's electrical engineering department. In 1953 the group completed an experimental computer using transistors instead of vacuum tubes. In 1954 the group completed MEG, which provided floating-point arithmetic (calculations using exponential notation—e.g., 3.27 ×

10[17]) and was manufactured by Ferranti as the Mercury beginning in 1957.

In 1956 Kilburn started his most ambitious project, MUSE, renamed Atlas when Ferranti joined the project in 1959. In parallel with two similar projects in the United States (LARC and Stretch) but largely independent of them, Atlas made the massive jump from running one program at a time to multiprogramming. With multiprogramming a computer can "interleave" several programs, allocating various computer resources (memory, storage, input, and output) to each program through an operating system. Atlas was also the first computer to employ a technique, now known as virtual memory or virtual storage, of using some slower external memory (such as magnetic drums) as though it were an extension of the computer's faster internal memory. Operational by 1962, Atlas was probably the most sophisticated computer of its time.

In 1964 Kilburn created the first department of computer science in the United Kingdom. In 1966 he started his last computer project, MU5. Operational by 1972, MU5 pioneered an architecture geared to the requirements of high-level languages (languages with more humanlike syntax).

Kilburn was made a professor in 1960 and was elected a fellow of the Royal Society in 1965. He retired in 1981.

STEPHANIE KWOLEK

(b. July 23, 1923, New Kensington, Pa., U.S.—d. June 18, 2014, Wilmington, Del.)

American chemist Stephanie Louise Kwolek was a pioneer in polymer research whose work yielded Kevlar, an ultrastrong and ultrathick material best known for its use in bulletproof vests.

Kwolek's father, a foundry worker, died when she was

10 years old, and her mother raised her and a brother alone. In 1946 she received a Bachelor of Science degree in chemistry from the Carnegie Institute of Technology (now Carnegie Mellon University), Pittsburgh, Pennsylvania. Intending eventually to go to medical school, she went to work as a laboratory chemist at the rayon department of the DuPont Company in Buffalo, New York. DuPont had introduced nylon just before World War II, and in the postwar years the company resumed its drive into the highly competitive market of synthetic fibers. Kwolek thus became engaged in basic research in a new and fast-growing field, and as a consequence she never left employment with DuPont. She moved with the company's Pioneering Research Laboratory to Wilmington, Delaware, in 1950 and retired with the rank of research associate in 1986. Having accumulated many patents and awards in her career, she continued in retirement to work as a consultant and public speaker.

Kwolek is best known for her work during the 1950s and '60s with aramids, or "aromatic polyamides," a type of polymer that can be made into strong, stiff, and flame-resistant fibers. Her laboratory work in aramids was conducted under the supervision of research fellow Paul W. Morgan, who calculated that the aramids would form stiff fibers owing to the presence of bulky benzene (or "aromatic") rings in their molecular chains but that they would have to be prepared from solution because they melt only at very high temperatures. Kwolek determined the solvents and polymerization conditions suitable for producing poly-m-phenylene isophthalamide, a compound that DuPont released in 1961 as a flame-resistant fiber with the trade name Nomex. She then extended her work into poly-p-benzamide and poly-p-phenylene terephthalamide, which she noted adopted highly regular rodlike molecular arrangements in solution. From these two "liquid crystal polymers" (the first ever prepared), fibers were spun that displayed unprecedented stiffness and tensile strength. Poly-p-phenylene terephthalamide was released commercially in 1971 with the trade name Kevlar, a fiber that finds use in high-strength tire cord, reinforced boat hulls and other structural parts, and lightweight bulletproof vests.

DOUGLAS ENGELBART

(b. Jan. 30, 1925, near Portland, Ore., U.S.—d. July 2, 2013, Atherton, Calif.)

Douglas Engelbart was an American inventor whose work beginning in the 1950s led to his patent for the computer mouse, the development of the basic graphical user interface, and groupware.

Engelbart grew up on a farm near Portland. Following two years of enlisted service as a radar technician for the U.S. Navy in World War II, he completed his bachelor's degree in electrical engineering at Oregon State University in 1948. He soon became dissatisfied with his electrical engineering job at the Ames Research Center, and in December 1950 had the inspiration that would drive the rest of his professional life.

Engelbart's dream was to use computers to connect individuals in a network that would allow them to share and update information in "real time." He combined this idea of collaborative software, or groupware, with his experience interpreting radar displays and with ideas he gleaned from an *Atlantic Monthly* article by Vannevar Bush, "As We May Think," to envision networked computers employing a graphical user interface. After receiving a Ph.D. in electrical engineering from the University of California at Berkeley in 1955, he stayed on as an acting assistant professor for a year before accepting a position with the Stanford Research Institute (SRI) in Stanford, California.

In 1963 Engelbart was given funding by SRI to start his own research laboratory, the Augmentation Research Center, where he worked on inventing and perfecting various devices—such as the computer mouse, the multiple window display, and hypermedia (the linking of texts, images, video, and sound files within a single document)—for inputting, manipulating, and displaying data. Together with a colleague at SRI, William English, he eventually perfected a variety of input devices—including joysticks, light pens, and track balls—that are now common. Prior to Engelbart's inventions, laborious and error-prone keypunch cards or manually set electronic switches were necessary to control computers, and data had to be printed before it could be viewed. His work made it possible for ordinary people to use computers.

Early in 1967 Engelbart's laboratory became the second site on the Advanced Research Projects Agency Network (ARPANET), the primary precursor to the internet. On December 9, 1968, at a computer conference in San Francisco, Engelbart demonstrated a working real-time collaborative computer system known as NLS (oNLine System). Using NLS, he and English (back at Stanford) worked on a shared document in one window (using keyboard and mouse input devices) while at the same time conducting the world's first public computer video conference in another window. Engelbart continued his research, building increasingly sophisticated input and display devices and improving the graphical user interface, but because of budget cuts at SRI most of his research staff migrated to other institutions such as Xerox Corporation's Palo Alto Research Center in Palo Alto, California.

In 1977 SRI sold Engelbart's NLS groupware system to Tymshare, Inc., a telephone networking company that renamed it Augment and sought to make it into a commercially viable office automation system. As the last remaining member of his research laboratory, and with SRI showing no further interest in his work, Engelbart joined Tymshare. In 1984 Tymshare was acquired by the McDonnell Douglas Corporation, where Engelbart worked on information systems. In 1989 he founded the Bootstrap Institute, a research and consulting firm. Over the following decade he finally began to receive recognition for his innovations, including the 1997 Turing Award, a major achievement in computer science.

ROBERT NOYCE

(b. Dec. 12, 1927, Burlington, Iowa, U.S.—d. June 3, 1990, Austin, Texas)

American engineer Robert Norton Noyce was coinventor of the integrated circuit, a system of interconnected transistors on a single silicon microchip.

Education

In 1939 the Noyce family moved to Grinnell, Iowa, where the father had accepted a position as a Congregational minister and where the son began to demonstrate the traits of an inventor and tinkerer. Noyce majored in physics at Grinnell College (B.A., 1949) and earned a doctorate in solid state physics from the Massachusetts Institute of Technology (MIT; Ph.D., 1953), for a dissertation related to the technology he found most fascinating, the transistor.

Shockley Semiconductor Laboratory

Developed at Bell Laboratories in 1947, the transistor had figured in Noyce's imagination since he saw an early one in a college physics class. In 1956, while working for Philco Corporation, Noyce met William Shockley, one of the transistor's Nobel Prize-winning inventors. Shockley was recruiting researchers for Shockley Semiconductor Laboratory, a company that he had started in Palo Alto, California, to produce high-speed transistors. Noyce jumped at the opportunity, renting a house in Palo Alto even before his official job interview.

By early 1957, however, engineers at the new company had rebelled and attempted to force Shockley out of his management position, arguing that his poor management delayed production and adversely affected morale. Noyce and seven colleagues, among them Gordon Moore, resigned after failing to remove Shockley. With Noyce as their leader, the group—labeled the "traitorous eight" by Shockley—successfully negotiated with the Fairchild Camera and Instrument Company to form a new company, Fairchild Semiconductor Corporation, located in Santa Clara.

Fairchild Semiconductor Corporation and the Integrated Circuit

In 1958 Jean Hoerni, another Fairchild Semiconductor founder, engineered a process to place a layer of silicon oxide on top of transistors, sealing out dirt, dust, and other contaminants. For Noyce, Hoerni's process made a fundamental innovation possible. At that time, Fairchild produced transistors and other elements on large silicon wafers, cut the components out of the wafer, and later connected individual components with wires. However, as the number of connections increased, it became progressively more difficult to solder in ever smaller spaces. Noyce realized that cutting the wafer apart was unnecessary; instead, he could manufacture an entire circuit—complete with transistors, resistors, and other elements—on a single silicon wafer, the integrated circuit (IC). In this sense, Noyce and coinventor Jack Kilby, who was working at Texas Instruments, Inc., thought along similar lines. They both saw the importance of the wafer, and each of their companies received patents on various aspects of IC design and manufacture. But Noyce saw further. Noyce saw that the solution to the problem of connecting the components was to evaporate lines of conductive metal (the "wires") directly onto the silicon wafer's surface, a technique known as the planar process. Kilby and Noyce share credit for independently inventing the integrated circuit. However, after much litigation, Fairchild Semiconductor was granted the patent on the planar process, the basic technique used by subsequent manufacturers. The patent made both inventors wealthy.

Intel Corporation

In 1968 Noyce and Moore left Fairchild Semiconductor to start their own company. Soon they were joined by Andrew Grove, another Fairchild colleague, and formed Intel Corporation. In 1971 Intel introduced the first microprocessor, which combined on a single silicon chip the circuitry for both information storage and information processing. Intel quickly became the leading producer of microprocessor chips.

Noyce served as president of Intel until 1975 and then as chairman of the board of directors before stepping down in 1978 to become chairman of the Semiconductor Industry Association (SIA).

Statesman

The SIA was formed to address the growing economic concerns of the American semiconductor industry, especially with respect to foreign competition. Noyce played an important role in establishing Sematech, a joint industry-government consortium formed with sometimes conflicting goals—research to keep the American semiconductor industry at the forefront and efforts to maintain a domestic semiconductor manufacturing capacity. Noyce became the first president of Sematech, Inc. in 1988.

Noyce held 16 patents and was awarded the National Medal of Science in 1979. A lifelong swimmer (and former Iowa state diving champion), Noyce died of a heart attack following a morning swim in 1990.

RON TOOMER

(b. May 31, 1930, Pasadena, Calif., U.S.—d. Sept. 26, 2011, Bedford, Tex.)

Ronald Valentine Toomer is an American engineer and roller coaster designer who could be considered the sovereign of steel coasters. His work with Arrow Dynamics (founded as Arrow Development Company in 1946) brought to life such influential steel thrillers as the tubular track Runaway Mine Ride (1966), the inverted helix-shaped Corkscrew (1975), and the first suspended coasters of the 1980s.

A mechanical engineering graduate of the University of Nevada–Reno (1961, B.S.), Toomer was involved in the first U.S. satellite launches and served on the team that designed the heat shield for the Apollo spacecraft. During his stint in the space program, Toomer met a coworker who had previously been a welder for the Arrow Development Company. In 1965 Toomer joined the company and was hired to work on the design of the Runaway Mine Ride, the world's first all-steel coaster. Toomer's tool of choice (and necessity): the slide rule. "A big part of the attraction of roller coasters is that people know that unlike with hang-gliding or skydiving, the train is definitely going to come back," Toomer said.

In more than 30 years in the amusement industry, Toomer designed more than 80 steel coasters worldwide. In 1975 he built one of the first looping coasters of the modern era—the Corkscrew at Knott's Berry Farm (Buena Park, California), which was followed the next year by one at Cedar Point (Sandusky, Ohio). The Corkscrew brought 360-degree rolls to coaster design for the first time. Other achievements by Toomer included Cedar Point's beloved Magnum XL-200 (1989), an out-and-back coaster that was the first to top 200 feet (60 m), and also the first suspended coasters, Big Bad Wolf (1984) at Busch Gardens, Williamsburg, Virginia, and Cedar Point's Iron Dragon (1987). All this time he gained fame for never riding his own creations, declaring, "I've had a bad motion sickness problem since I was a little kid. But I've ridden enough of them to know what happens and how it feels."

Toomer became president of Arrow Dynamics in 1986, at about the time that the company was developing the innovative Pipeline coaster, on which the cars execute a snap roll of 182 degrees around their longitudinal axis. Unfortunately, the highly complex project ran out of funds before it could be realized as anything more than a prototype. In the 1990s Toomer held posts as chairman of the board and as director. In 2000 he was inducted into the International Association of Amusement Parks and Attractions Hall of Fame.

HEINRICH ROHRER AND GERD BINNIG

respectively, (b. June 6, 1933, Buchs, Sankt Gallen canton, Switz.—d. May 16, 2013, Wollerau); (b. July 20, 1947, Frankfurt am Main, W.Ger.)

The scanning tunneling microscope (STM) appeared in 1981 when Swiss physicists Gerd Binnig and Heinrich Rohrer set out to build a tool for studying the local conductivity of surfaces. Its principle of operation is based on the quantum mechanical phenomenon known as tunneling, in which the wavelike properties of electrons permit them to "tunnel" beyond the surface of a solid into regions of space that are forbidden to them under the rules of classical physics. The probability of finding such tunneling electrons decreases exponentially as the distance from the surface increases. The STM makes use of this extreme sensitivity to distance. The sharp tip of a tungsten needle is positioned a few angstroms from the sample surface. A small voltage is applied between the probe tip and the surface, causing electrons to tunnel across the gap. As the probe is scanned over the surface, it registers variations in the tunneling current, and this information can be processed to provide a topographical image of the surface.

Binnig and Rohrer chose the surface of gold for their first image. When the image was displayed on the screen of a television monitor, they saw rows of precisely spaced atoms and observed broad terraces separated by steps one atom in height. Binnig and Rohrer had discovered in the STM a simple method for creating a direct image of the atomic structure of surfaces. Their discovery opened a new era for surface science, and their impressive achievement was recognized with the award of half the Nobel Prize for Physics in 1986. (Ernst Ruska, a German electrical engineer who invented the electron microscope, received the other half of the prize.)

Heinrich Rohrer

Heinrich Rohrer was educated at the Swiss Federal Institute of Technology in Zürich and received his Ph.D. there in 1960. In 1963, after a period of postdoctoral work at Rutgers University in New Jersey, he joined the IBM Zürich Research Laboratory, where he remained until his retirement in 1997. Binnig also joined the laboratory, and it was there that the two men designed and built the first STM. This instrument is equipped with a tiny tungsten probe whose tip, only about one or two atoms wide, is brought to within five or ten atoms' distance of the surface of a conducting or semiconducting material. (An atom is equal to about one angstrom, or one ten-billionth of a meter.) When the electric potential of the tip is made to differ by a few volts from that of the surface, quantum mechanical effects cause a measurable electric current to cross the gap. The strength of this current is extremely sensitive to the distance between the probe and the surface, and as the probe's tip scans the surface, it can be kept a fixed distance away by raising and lowering it so as to hold the current constant. A record of the elevation of the probe is a topographical map of the surface under study, on which the contour intervals are so small that the individual atoms making up the surface are clearly recognizable.

Gerd Binnig

The German-born Gerd Binnig graduated from Johann Wolfgang Goethe University in Frankfurt in 1973 and received a doctorate from the University of Frankfurt in 1978. He then joined the IBM Zürich Research Laboratory, where he and Rohrer designed and built the first STM. In 1985–86 Binnig joined a physics research group at IBM's Almaden Research Center in San Jose, California, and in 1987–95 he directed an IBM research group at the University of Munich. He then returned to Zürich.

About the time Binnig shared the Nobel Prize with Rohrer for the invention of the STM, he developed the concept of atomic force microscopy. An atomic force microscope profiles a sample by dragging a stylus only a few atoms wide across the surface of the sample and measuring the force between the stylus and the surface. The resulting signal can be translated into a description of the surface topography. This surface-force scan can be converted into a three-dimensional surface image.

Binnig's involvement in the invention of the STM stimulated an interest in the creative process. In 1989 he published the book *Aus dem Nichts* ("Out of Nothing"), which posited that creativity grows from disorder. Binnig went on to articulate what he called "fractal Darwinism," a theory that new ideas or devices evolve through complex interactions on multiple scales, from the social group to the individual and from broad concepts to specific problems.

PAUL LAUTERBUR AND PETER MANSFIELD

respectively, (b. May 6, 1929, Sidney, Ohio, U.S.—d. March 27, 2007, Urbana, Ill.); (b. Oct. 9, 1933, London, Eng.—d. Feb. 8, 2017)

The 2003 Nobel Prize for Physiology or Medicine was awarded to two pioneers of magnetic resonance imaging (MRI), a computerized scanning technology that produces images of internal body structures, especially those comprising soft tissues. The recipients were chemist Paul Lauterbur of the University of Illinois at Urbana-Champaign and physicist Sir Peter Mansfield of the University of Nottingham, England.

"A great advantage with MRI is that it is harmless according to all present knowledge," stated the Nobel Assembly at the Karolinska Institute in Stockholm, which awarded the prize. Unlike X-ray and computed tomography (CT) examinations, MRI avoided the use of potentially harmful ionizing radiation; rather, it produced its images with magnetic fields and radio waves. MRI scans spared patients not only many X-ray examinations but also surgical procedures and invasive tests formerly needed to diagnose diseases and follow up after treatments. More than 60 million MRI procedures were performed in 2002 alone, according to the Nobel Assembly.

Paul Lauterbur

Paul Christian Lauterbur received a Ph.D. in chemistry from the University of Pittsburgh in 1962. He served as a professor at the University of New York at Stony Brook from 1969 to 1985, when he accepted the position of professor at the University of Illinois at Urbana-Champaign and became director of its Biomedical Magnetic Resonance Laboratory.

Lauterbur began work in the early 1970s, when the technology underpinning MRI was a laboratory research tool. Called nuclear magnetic resonance (NMR) spectroscopy, it involves putting a sample to be analyzed in a strong magnetic field and then irradiating it with weak radio waves at the appropriate frequency. In the presence of the magnetic field, the nuclei of certain atoms—for example, ordinary hydrogen—absorb the radio energy; i.e., they show resonance at that particular frequency. Because the resonance frequency depends on the kind of nuclei and is influenced by the presence of nearby atoms, absorption measurements (absorption signal spectra) can provide information about the molecular structure of various solids and liquids. When the nuclei return to their previous energy levels, they emit energy, which carries additional information. NMR spectroscopy has remained a key tool in chemical analysis.

When studying molecules with NMR, chemists always had tried to maintain a steady magnetic field because variations made the absorption signals fuzzy. Lauterbur realized that if the magnetic field was deliberately made nonuniform, information contained in the signal distortions could be used to create two-dimensional images of a sample's internal structure. While at Stony Brook, he worked evenings developing his idea, using an NMR unit borrowed from campus chemists. His discovery laid the groundwork for the development of MRI as Mansfield transformed Lauterbur's work into a medical tool.

Peter Mansfield

Peter Mansfield received a Ph.D. in physics from the University of London in 1962. Following two years as a research associate in the United States, he joined the faculty of the University of Nottingham, where he became professor in 1979. Mansfield was knighted in 1993.

Mansfield's prize-winning work expanded upon Lauterbur's earlier discoveries regarding NMR. MRI imaging succeeds because the human body is about two-thirds water, whose molecules are made of hydrogen and oxygen atoms. There are differences in the amount of water present in different organs and tissues. In addition, the amount of water often changes when body structures become injured or diseased; those variations show up in

MRI images. When the body is exposed to MRI's magnetic field and its pulses of radio waves, the nucleus of each hydrogen atom in water absorbs energy; it then emits the energy in the form of radio waves, or resonance signals, as it returns to its previous energy level. Electronic devices detect the myriad resonance signals from all the hydrogen nuclei in the tissue being examined, and computer processing builds cross-sectional images of internal body structures, based on differences in water content and movements of water molecules. Computer processing also can stack the cross sections in sequence to create three-dimensional, solid images. Because MRI does not have the harmful side effects of X-ray or computed tomography (CT) examinations and is noninvasive, the technology proved an invaluable tool in medicine.

Mansfield's research helped transform Lauterbur's discoveries into a practical technology in medicine by developing a way of using the nonuniformities, or gradients, introduced in the magnetic field to identify differences in the resonance signals more precisely. He also created new mathematical methods for quickly analyzing information in the signal and showed how to attain extremely rapid imaging.

ROBERT KAHN AND VINT CERF

respectively, (b. Dec. 23, 1938, Brooklyn, N.Y., U.S.); (b. June 23, 1943, New Haven, Conn., U.S.)

The internet grew out of funding by the U.S. Advanced Research Projects Agency (ARPA), later renamed the Defense Advanced Research Projects Agency (DARPA), to develop a communication system among government and academic computer-research laboratories. First, DARPA established a program to investigate the interconnection of "heterogeneous networks." This program, called Internetting, was based on the newly introduced concept of open architecture networking, in which networks with defined standard interfaces would be interconnected by "gateways."

In order for the concept to work, a new protocol had to be designed and developed; indeed, a system architecture was also required. In 1974 computer scientist Vint Cerf, then at Stanford University in California, and electrical engineer Robert Kahn, then at DARPA, collaborated on a paper that first described such a protocol and system architecture—namely, the transmission control protocol (TCP), which enabled different types of machines on networks all over the world to route and assemble data packets. TCP, which originally included the Internet protocol (IP), a global addressing mechanism that allowed routers to get data packets to their ultimate destination, formed the TCP/IP standard, which was adopted by the U.S. Department of Defense in 1980. TCP/IP is now the standard internet communications protocol that allows digital computers to communicate over long distances. In acknowledgement of their role as two of the principal architects of the internet, Kahn and Cerf received the 2004 A.M. Turing Award from the Association for Computing Machinery.

Robert Kahn

After receiving an engineering degree from City College of New York in 1960, Robert Elliot Kahn received his M.A. (1962) and Ph.D. (1964) in electrical engineering from Princeton University. Immediately after completing his doctorate, Kahn worked for Bell Laboratories and subsequently served as an assistant professor of electrical engineering at the Massachusetts Institute of

Technology (MIT) from 1964 to 66. However, it was his role as a senior scientist at Bolt Beranek & Newman (BB&N), an engineering consulting firm located in Cambridge, Massachusetts, that brought Kahn into contact with the planning for a new kind of computer network, the Advanced Research Project Network (ARPANET).

ARPANET was named for its sponsor, the Defense Advanced Research Projects Agency, or DARPA. The network was based on a radically different architecture known as packet switching, in which messages were split into multiple "packets" that traveled independently over many different circuits to their common destination. But the ARPANET was more than a predecessor to the internet—it was the common technological context in which an entire generation of computer scientists came of age. While at BB&N, Kahn had two major accomplishments. First, he was part of a group that designed the network's Interface Message Processor, which would mediate between the network and each institution's host computer. Second, and perhaps more important, in 1972 Kahn helped organize the first International Conference on Computer Communication, which served as the ARPANET's public debut.

In 1972 Kahn left BB&N for DARPA's Information Processing Techniques Office (IPTO). Here he confronted a set of problems related to the deployment of packet switching technology in military radio and satellite communications. However, the real technical problem lay in connecting these disparate military networks—hence the name internet for a network of networks. As program manager and later director of the IPTO, Kahn worked closely with Cerf and others on the development of the internet's technical protocol, TCP/IP, which separated packet error checking (TCP) from issues related to domains and destinations (IP). The protocol is the basis for the internet's open architecture, which permits any computer with the appropriate connection to enter the network. In addition to his work on the internet, Kahn was the designer of the U.S. military's Strategic Computing Initiative during the administration of President Ronald Reagan. Kahn also coined the phrase "national information infrastructure" during this period.

Upon leaving IPTO in 1985, Kahn served as president of the Corporation for the National Research Initiatives, a not-for-profit group located in Reston, Virginia, and dedicated to the development of network technologies for the public. In 2001 he was among four individuals honored by the National Academy of Engineering with the Charles Stark Draper Prize to recognize his role in developing the internet.

Vint Cerf

In 1965 Vinton Gray Cerf received his bachelor's degree in mathematics from Stanford University, California, U.S. He then worked for IBM as a systems engineer before attending the University of California at Los Angeles (UCLA), where he earned a master's degree in computer science in 1970. He returned to Stanford and completed his doctorate in computer science in 1972.

While at UCLA, Cerf wrote the communication protocol for the ARPANET, the first computer network based on packet switching, a heretofore untested technology. (In contrast to ordinary telephone communications, in which a specific circuit must be dedicated to the transmission, packet switching splits a message into "packets" that travel independently over many different circuits.) UCLA was among the four original ARPANET nodes. While working on the protocol, Cerf met Kahn, an electrical engineer who was then a senior scientist at Bolt Beranek & Newman. Cerf's professional relationship with Kahn was among the most important of his career.

In 1972 Kahn moved to DARPA as a program manager in the IPTO, where he began to envision a network of packet-switching networks—essentially, what would become the internet. In 1973 Kahn approached Cerf, then a professor at Stanford, to assist him in designing this new network. Cerf and Kahn soon worked out a preliminary version of what they called the ARPA Internet, the details of which they published as a joint paper in 1974. Cerf joined Kahn at IPTO in 1976 to manage the office's networking projects. Together they produced TCP/IP, an electronic transmission protocol that separated packet error checking (TCP) from issues related to domains and destinations (IP).

Cerf's work on making the internet a publicly accessible medium continued after he left DARPA in 1982 to become a vice president at MCI Communications Corporation (after 1998, WorldCom, Inc.). While at MCI he led the effort to develop and deploy MCI Mail, the first commercial email service to use the internet. In 1986 Cerf became a vice president at the Corporation for National Research Initiatives, a not-for-profit corporation located in Reston, Virginia, that Kahn, as president, had formed to develop network-based information technologies for the public good. Cerf also served as founding president of the Internet Society from 1992 to 1995. In 1994 Cerf returned to WorldCom as a senior vice president, and in 1998 he became the first chairman of the Internet Corporation for Assigned Names and Numbers, the group that oversees the internet's growth and expansion.

In addition to his work on the internet, Cerf served on many government panels related to cyber-security and the national information infrastructure. A fan of science fiction, he was a technical consultant to one of author Gene Roddenbury's posthumous television projects, *Earth: Final Conflict*. Among his many honors is the National Academy of Engineering's Charles Stark Draper Prize (2001).

IAN WILMUT

(b. July 7, 1944, Hampton Lucy, Warwickshire, Eng.—d. Sept. 10, 2023)

Sir Ian Wilmut is an English developmental biologist who was the first to use nuclear transfer of differentiated adult cells to generate a mammalian clone, a Finn Dorset sheep named Dolly, born in 1996.

Education and Cryopreservation Research

Wilmut was raised in Coventry, a town in the historic English county of Warwickshire, and he attended the Agricultural College at the University of Nottingham. In his undergraduate studies, Wilmut initially pursued his lifelong interest in farming, particularly in raising animals such as sheep. However, he soon turned his attention to animal science and basic research. In 1966, his final year at Nottingham, he received a scholarship to conduct research for a summer under English biologist Ernest John Christopher Polge in the Unit of Reproductive Physiology and Biochemistry, then a division of the Agricultural Research Council at the University of Cambridge. During this time, Wilmut performed basic experiments on animal embryos. Following his graduation from Nottingham in 1967, he returned to Cambridge, where he pursued a doctorate under the guidance of Polge, whose research was focused on improving methods of embryo cryopreservation. In 1971 Wilmut was awarded a doctorate by Darwin College, Cambridge; the title of his thesis was "Deep Freeze Preservation of Boar Semen." Wilmut remained at Cambridge and conducted extensive research on the cryopreservation of embryos. In 1973 he successfully implanted into a surrogate cow a calf embryo that had been cryopreserved. The embryo was carried to term, and Wilmut named the first-ever "frozen calf" Frostie.

GENETIC ENGINEERING AND CLONING RESEARCH

PHARMING

In 1973 Wilmut was appointed senior scientific officer at the Animal Breeding Research Organisation (ABRO; renamed Edinburgh Research Station of the Institute of Animal Physiology and Genetics Research in 1985 and finally Roslin Institute in 1993), a government-supported research facility located in Roslin, Scotland, just south of Edinburgh. At the ABRO facility, Wilmut studied embryo development and became interested in the underlying causes of embryo death in mammals. However, in the early 1980s, changes in ABRO leadership and a shift in the focus of government research projects forced Wilmut into the realm of genetic engineering. The new goal of ABRO was to generate sheep genetically engineered to produce large quantities of human proteins that would be suitable for therapeutic uses, a pursuit that came to be known as "pharming." Although Wilmut had little experience with genetic engineering and had limited enthusiasm for the project, he used his knowledge of developmental biology to obtain zygotes (one-celled embryos) from sheep and developed techniques to inject DNA into the zygote pronucleus (a haploid nucleus occurring in embryos prior to fertilization). This work eventually led to the generation of a sheep named Tracy. Tracy was created from a zygote genetically engineered through DNA injection to produce milk containing large quantities of the human enzyme alpha-1 antitrypsin, a substance used to treat cystic fibrosis and emphysema.

Nuclear Transfer

Wilmut's initial forays into cloning began in the late 1980s with embryonic stem cells. Wilmut and his colleagues were interested primarily in nuclear transfer, a technique first conceived in 1928 by German embryologist Hans Spemann. Nuclear transfer involves the introduction of the nucleus from a cell into an enucleated egg cell (an egg cell that has had its own nucleus removed). This can be accomplished through fusion of the cell to the egg (the technique that Wilmut used in all his later cloning experiments) or through the removal of the nucleus from the cell and the subsequent transplantation of that nucleus into the enucleated egg cell (a technique refined in the early 2000s). In 1989 Wilmut and Lawrence Smith, a graduate student conducting his thesis research at Roslin, generated four cloned lambs by using embryonic cell nuclear transfer, in which the nucleus from an embryonic stem cell was inserted into an enucleated egg. This research led Wilmut and Smith to an important discovery—namely, that the stage of the cell cycle (the sequence through which each cell progresses from one cell division to the next) at the time of nuclear transfer determined the success or failure of the experiment. They realized that the four clones they had generated happened by chance.

In 1991 Wilmut hired English biologist Keith Campbell (Smith had left the research center in 1990), whose knowledge of the cell cycle proved instrumental in advancing the technique of nuclear transfer developed at Roslin. Wilmut and Campbell's first major success came in 1995, with the generation of two cloned Welsh mountain sheep, Megan and Morag. The following year Wilmut, Campbell, and their team of scientists decided to test a new theory based on the idea that the age or the stage of differentiation of a donor cell did not matter in nuclear transfer. Prior to this theory, nuclear transfer was believed to work only if the nucleus used as the donor for nuclear transfer came from a cell that was totipotent—i.e., having the ability to differentiate into any type of cell in the body and therefore possessing no characteristics of differentiation itself. However, observations from laboratory experiments and from Megan and Morag, who were produced using nine-day-old embryonic cells, which are presumably less totipotent than younger embryonic cells, indicated that an enucleated host egg could somehow reverse the differentiation of the donor cell nucleus, converting it back to a state of totipotency or pluripotency (slightly more differentiated than a totipotent cell). This led to the idea of using the nucleus from an already differentiated adult cell as a donor nucleus.

Dolly and Polly

During the winter of 1995–96, Wilmut was involved in three pivotal cloning experiments conducted at Roslin. In the first, Wilmut and his team of scientists performed embryonic cell nuclear transfer by using cultured embryonic cells that were nine days old. This was similar to the experiment that led to the creation of Megan and Morag. However, the new experiment involved a different sheep breed; the cells used for nuclear transfer came from a Poll Dorset sheep. This first experiment resulted in the birth in 1996 of four Poll Dorset clones: Cedric, Cecil, Cyril, and

Tuppence. In the second experiment, the team used fetal fibroblasts isolated from sheep fetuses after 26 days of development; these cells served as nucleus donors for transfer into an enucleated egg. This experiment resulted in the birth of two clones, Taffy and Tweed. In the third experiment, the scientists isolated adult cells (in this case, mammary gland cells) from a six-year-old ewe and used these cells as nucleus donors for transfer into egg cells; this technique inspired the later development of a procedure called somatic cell nuclear transfer (SCNT). Wilmut and his team constructed 277 embryos containing adult cell nuclei that were implanted into 13 surrogate mothers, only one of which became pregnant. This pregnancy was carried to term successfully. The Finn Dorset lamb, born on July 5, 1996, was Dolly.

In 1997, following the publication in the journal *Nature* of a summary of their research leading to Dolly, Wilmut, Campbell, and the Roslin Institute instantly became known for having opened the door to a new era of controversial cloning research. The cloning of Dolly generated speculation in the media and in the scientific community about the possibility of cloning humans. Wilmut considered human cloning impractical for both ethical and scientific reasons. From his work with sheep, he knew the dangers of cloning; many embryos died following implantation, and those embryos that survived and developed to term as full-grown fetuses sometimes died immediately following birth or were born with birth defects.

Wilmut was not interested in cloning simply for the sake of producing cloned animals, and neither was his team of scientists at Roslin. They still had problems to solve concerning their work on pharming. In 1997 Wilmut and his colleagues generated Polly, a Poll Dorset clone made from nuclear transfer using a fetal fibroblast nucleus genetically engineered to express a human gene known as

FIX. This gene encodes a substance called human factor IX, a clotting factor that occurs naturally in most people but is absent in people with hemophilia, who require replacement therapy with a therapeutic form of the substance. Polly—along with two other sheep engineered to produce human factor IX that also were born in 1997—represented a major advance in pharming. The successful birth of Polly marked Wilmut's last major cloning experiment.

Later Career

Throughout Wilmut's career at Roslin, he had been slowly moving away from research relying on embryonic stem cells, primarily because culturing embryonic stem cells from sheep embryos was extraordinarily difficult and impractical in terms of cost and time. In 2000 Wilmut was promoted to head of the department of gene expression and development at the Roslin Institute, and his research interests shifted from animals to humans. He was particularly interested in uncovering the genetic mechanisms that control embryonic development and the role that these mechanisms play in human disease. In 2005 he accepted a position as chair of reproductive science at the University of Edinburgh. He maintained a relationship with the Roslin Institute, acting as a visiting scientist. Wilmut also directed the Medical Research Council's Centre for Regenerative Medicine, located in Edinburgh, and led research efforts into cellular reprogramming.

Wilmut received several awards during his career, including the Ernst Schering Prize in 2002 and the Paul Ehrlich and Ludwig Darmstaedter Prize in 2005. Wilmut also was made fellow of the Royal Society of Edinburgh in 2000 and of the Royal Society of London in 2002; he was knighted in 2007. In addition to papers published in high-ranking journals such as *Nature* and *Science*, Wilmut also published several books, including *The Second Creation: Dolly and the Age of Biological Control* (2000; with Keith Campbell and Colin Tudge) and *After Dolly: The Uses and Misuses of Human Cloning* (2006; with Roger Highfield).

RODNEY BROOKS

(b. Dec. 30, 1954, Adelaide, South Australia, Austl.)

Rodney Allen Brooks is an Australian-born computer scientist, artificial intelligence scientist, and designer of mobile autonomous robots.

While attending Flinders University in Adelaide, where he received his bachelor's (1975) and master's degrees (1978) in pure mathematics, Brooks was given access to the university's mainframe computer for 12 hours each Sunday. This experience with computers was enough to convince Brooks to come to America to study with the artificial intelligence (AI) pioneer John McCarthy at Stanford University, California. Brooks chose a traditional AI problem for his doctoral research (1981), which he subsequently expanded and published as *Model-Based Computer Vision* (1984).

By the time Brooks had finished his doctorate and moved to the Mobile Robotics Laboratory at the Massachusetts Institute of Technology (MIT) in 1984, he had become discouraged with AI research, especially with the field's top-down approach to problem solving. The top-down approach, which dominated the field at that time, presupposes that a computer must first be supplied with an internal representation of the "essential" features of the world in which it operates—an immensely difficult framework problem for all but the very simplest tasks.

Brooks turned this approach on its head, arguing that research should focus on a bottom-up approach—that is, on action and behavior rather than on representation and function. Brooks began by building basic robots that could perform the simplest "insect-like" actions. Although no one claims that insects have sophisticated brains, they can engage in rather elaborate behaviors. Similarly, building on a few simple actions and the premise that learning comes from interacting with the real world rather than any model, Brooks's robots displayed surprisingly complex behavior.

In 1997 Brooks became director of the MIT Artificial Intelligence Research Laboratory, where he continued to push AI in this fundamentally new direction. His influential and accessible essays were collected in *Cambrian Intelligence: The Early History of the New AI* (1999). What initially had appeared heretical to traditional AI eventually became a new orthodoxy, complete with industrial and military applications. Brooks and his students designed robots to explore Mars, as well as for more mundane tasks such as clearing minefields.

Brooks went on to the project of "raising" a robot "child" named Cog—a clever allusion to cognition and gears. Ironically, in abandoning AI's traditional attempts to model human intelligence, Brooks and Cog hold out the possibility of redefining what it means to be human and intelligent.

STEVE JOBS AND STEPHEN WOZNIAK

respectively, (b. Feb. 24, 1955, San Francisco, Calif., U.S.—d. Oct. 5, 2011); (b. Aug. 11, 1950, San Jose, Calif., U.S.)

Like the founding of the early chip companies and the invention of the microprocessor, the story of Apple is a key part of Silicon Valley folklore. Two whiz kids, Stephen G. Wozniak and Steven P. Jobs, shared an interest in electronics. Wozniak purchased one of the early microprocessors, the Mostek 6502, and used it to design a computer. When Hewlett-Packard, where "Woz" had an internship, declined to build his design, Jobs suggested that they could sell it together. The product, which they called the Apple I, was actually only a printed circuit board. It lacked a case, a keyboard, and a power supply. To raise the capital to buy the parts they needed, Jobs sold his minibus and Wozniak his calculator, and they set up production in Jobs's parents' garage. From these beginnings sprang one of the leading personal computer companies in the world. In 1980 Apple Computer, Inc., announced its first public stock offering, and its young founders became instant millionaires.

Steve Jobs

Steven Paul Jobs, cofounder of Apple Computer, Inc. (now Apple, Inc.), was a charismatic pioneer of the personal computer era.

Founding of Apple

Jobs was raised by adoptive parents in Cupertino, California, located in what is now known as Silicon Valley. Though he was interested in engineering, his passions of youth varied. He dropped out of Reed College, in Portland, Oregon, took a job at Atari Corporation as a video game designer in early 1974, and saved enough money for a pilgrimage to India to experience Buddhism.

Back in Silicon Valley in the autumn of 1974, Jobs reconnected with Stephen Wozniak, a former high school

Steve Jobs (1955–2011) helped pioneer revolutionary shifts in the capabilities of personal computers.

friend who was working for the Hewlett-Packard Company. When Wozniak told Jobs of his progress in designing his own computer logic board, Jobs suggested that they go into business together, which they did after Hewlett-Packard formally turned down Wozniak's design in 1976. The Apple I, as they called the logic board, was built in the Jobses' family garage.

Jobs was one of the first entrepreneurs to understand that the personal computer would appeal to a broad audience, at least if it did not appear to belong in a junior high school science fair. With Jobs's encouragement, Wozniak designed an improved model, the Apple II, complete with a keyboard, and they arranged to have a sleek, molded plastic case manufactured to enclose the unit.

Though Jobs had long, unkempt hair and eschewed business garb, he managed to obtain financing, distribution, and publicity for the company, Apple Computer, incorporated in 1977—the same year that the Apple II was completed. The machine was an immediate success, becoming synonymous with the boom in personal computers. In 1981 the company had a record-setting public stock offering and, in 1983, made the quickest entrance (to that time) into the *Fortune* 500 list of America's top companies. In 1983 the company recruited PepsiCo, Inc., president John Sculley to be its chief executive officer (CEO) and, implicitly, Jobs's mentor in the fine points of running a large corporation. Jobs had convinced Sculley to accept the position by challenging him: "Do you want to sell sugar water for the rest of your life?" The line was shrewdly effective, but it also revealed Jobs's own near-messianic belief in the computer revolution.

Insanely Great

During that same period, Jobs was heading the most important project in the company's history. In 1979 he led a small group of Apple engineers to a technology demonstration at the Xerox Corporation's Palo Alto Research Center (PARC) to see how the graphical user interface could make computers easier to use and more efficient. Soon afterward, Jobs left the engineering team that was designing Lisa, a business computer, to head a smaller group building a lower-cost computer. Both computers were redesigned to exploit and refine the PARC ideas, but Jobs was explicit in favoring the Macintosh, or Mac, as the new computer became known. Jobs coddled his engineers and referred to them as artists, but his style was uncompromising; at one point he demanded a redesign of an internal circuit board simply because he considered it unattractive. He would later be renowned for his insistence that the Macintosh be not merely great but "insanely great." In January 1984 Jobs himself introduced the Macintosh in a brilliantly choreographed demonstration that was the centerpiece of an extraordinary publicity campaign. It would later be pointed to as the archetype of "event marketing."

However, the first Macs were underpowered and expensive, and they had few software applications—all of which resulted in disappointing sales. Apple steadily improved the machine, so that it eventually became the company's lifeblood as well as the model for all subsequent computer interfaces. But Jobs's apparent failure to correct the problem quickly led to tensions in the company, and in 1985 Sculley convinced Apple's board of directors to remove the company's famous cofounder.

NeXT and Pixar

Jobs quickly started another firm, the NeXT Corporation, designing powerful workstation computers for the education market. His funding partners included Texan entrepreneur Ross Perot and Canon, Inc., a Japanese electronics company. Although the NeXT computer was notable for its engineering design, it was eclipsed by less costly computers from competitors such as Sun Microsystems, Inc. In the early 1990s, Jobs focused the company on its innovative software system, NeXTStep.

Meanwhile, in 1986 Jobs bought Pixar Animation Studios, a computer-graphics firm founded by Hollywood movie director George Lucas. Over the following decade Jobs built Pixar into a major animation studio that, among other achievements, produced the first full-length feature film to be completely computer-animated, *Toy Story*, in 1995. Also in 1995, Pixar's public stock offering made Jobs, for the first time, a billionaire.

Saving Apple

In late 1996, Apple, saddled by huge financial losses and on the verge of collapse, hired a new chief executive, semiconductor executive Gilbert Amelio. When Amelio learned that the company, following intense and prolonged research efforts, had failed to develop an acceptable replacement for the Macintosh's aging operating system (OS), he chose NeXTStep, buying Jobs's company for more than $400 million—and bringing Jobs back to Apple as a consultant. However, Apple's board of directors soon became disenchanted with Amelio's inability to turn the company's finances around and in June 1997 requested Apple's prodigal cofounder to lead the company once again. Jobs quickly forged an alliance with Apple's erstwhile foe, the Microsoft Corporation, scrapped Amelio's Mac-clone agreements, and simplified the company's product line. He also engineered an award-winning advertising campaign that urged potential customers to "think different" and buy Macintoshes. Just as important is what he did not do: he resisted the temptation to make machines that ran Microsoft's Windows OS; nor did he, as some urged, spin off Apple as a software-only company. Jobs believed that Apple, as the only major personal computer maker with its own operating system, was in a unique position to innovate.

Innovate he did. In 1998, Jobs introduced the iMac, an egg-shaped, one-piece computer that offered high-speed processing at a relatively modest price and initiated a trend of high-fashion computers. (Subsequent models sported five different bright colors.) By the end of the year, the iMac was the nation's highest-selling personal computer, and Jobs was able to announce consistent profits for the once-moribund company. The following year, he triumphed once more with the stylish iBook, a laptop computer built with students in mind, and the G4, a desktop computer sufficiently powerful that (so Apple boasted) it could not be exported under certain circumstances because it qualified as a supercomputer. Though Apple did not regain the industry dominance it once had, Steve Jobs had saved his company, and in the process reestablished himself as a master high-technology marketer and visionary.

Reinventing Apple

In 2001 Jobs started reinventing Apple for the 21st century. That was the year that Apple introduced iTunes, a computer program for playing music and for converting music to the compact MP3 digital format commonly used in computers and other digital devices. Later the same year, Apple began selling the iPod, a portable MP3 player, which quickly became the market leader. In 2003 Apple began selling downloadable copies of major record company songs in MP3 format over the internet. By 2006 more than one billion songs and videos had been sold through Apple's online iTunes Store. In recognition of the growing shift in the company's business, Jobs officially changed the name of the company to Apple, Inc., on January 9, 2007.

In 2007 Jobs took the company into the telecommunications business with the introduction of the touch-screen iPhone, a mobile telephone with capabilities for playing MP3s and videos and for accessing the internet. Later that year, Apple introduced the iPod Touch, a portable MP3 and gaming device that included built-in Wi-Fi and an iPhone-like touch screen. Bolstered by the use of the iTunes Store to sell Apple and third-party software, the iPhone and iPod Touch soon boasted more games than any other portable gaming system. Jobs announced in 2008 that future releases of the iPhone and iPod Touch would offer improved game functionality. In an ironic development, Apple, which had not supported game developers in its early years out of fear of its computers not being taken seriously as business machines, was now staking a claim to a greater role in the gaming business to go along with its move into telecommunications.

Health Issues

In 2003 Jobs was diagnosed with a rare form of pancreatic cancer. He put off surgery for about nine months while he tried alternative medicine approaches. In 2004 he underwent major reconstructive surgery, known as the Whipple operation. During the procedure, part of the pancreas, a portion of the bile duct, the gallbladder, and the duodenum are removed, after which what is left of the pancreas, the bile duct, and the intestine is reconnected to direct the gastrointestinal secretions back into the stomach. Following a short recovery, Jobs returned to running Apple.

Throughout 2008 Jobs lost significant weight, which produced considerable speculation that his cancer was back. Perhaps more than those of any other large corporation, Apple's stock market shares were tied to the health of its CEO, which led to demands by investors for full disclosure of his health. On January 9, 2009, Jobs released a statement that he was being treated for a hormonal imbalance and that he would continue his corporate duties. Less than a week later, however, he announced that he was taking an immediate leave of absence through the end of June in order to recover his health. Having removed himself, at least temporarily, from the corporate structure, Jobs resumed his stance that his health was a private matter and refused to disclose any more details. In June it was reported that Jobs had received a liver transplant the previous April. Not disclosed was whether the pancreatic cancer he had been treated for previously had spread to his liver. Jobs came back to work on June 29, 2009. In January 2011, however, Jobs took another medical leave of absence. In August he resigned as CEO but became chairman. He died two months later.

Stephen Wozniak

Stephen Gary Wozniak, an American electronics engineer, was cofounder, with Steven P. Jobs, of Apple Computer, Inc., and designer of the first commercially successful personal computer.

Wozniak—or "Woz," as he was commonly known—was the son of an electrical engineer for the Lockheed Missiles and Space Company in Sunnyvale, California, in what would become known as Silicon Valley. A precocious but undisciplined student with a gift for mathematics and an interest in electronics, he attended the University of Colorado at Boulder for one year (1968–69) before dropping out. Following his return to California, he attended a local community college and then the University of California, Berkeley. In 1971 Wozniak designed the "Blue Box," a device for phreaking (hacking into the telephone network without paying for long-distance calls) that he and Jobs, a student at his old high school whom he met about this time, began selling to other students. Also during the early 1970s Wozniak worked at several small electronics firms in the San Francisco Bay area before obtaining a position with the Hewlett-Packard Company in 1975, by which time he had formally dropped out of Berkeley.

Wozniak also became involved with the Homebrew Computer Club, a San Francisco Bay area group centered around the Altair 8800 microcomputer do-it-yourself kit, which was based on one of the world's first microprocessors, the Intel Corporation 8080, released in 1975. While working as an engineering intern at Hewlett-Packard, Wozniak designed his own microcomputer in 1976 using the new microprocessor, but the company was not interested in developing his design. Jobs, who was also a Homebrew member, showed so much enthusiasm for Wozniak's design that they decided to work together, forming their own company, Apple Computer. Their initial capital came from selling Jobs's automobile and Wozniak's programmable calculator, and they set up production in the Jobs family garage to build microcomputer circuit boards. Sales of the kit were promising, so they decided to produce a finished product, the Apple II; completed in 1977, it included a built-in keyboard and support for a color monitor. The Apple II, which combined Wozniak's brilliant engineering with Jobs's aesthetic sense, was the first personal computer to appeal beyond hobbyist circles. When the company went public in 1980, its market value exceeded $1 billion, at the time the fastest rise to that milestone in corporate history, and Wozniak's stock in the company made him an instant multimillionaire.

During these years, Wozniak designed new hardware components, such as the 3.5-inch (8.9-cm) floppy disk drive for the Apple II, and various components of the Apple operating system and its software applications. This work ended in 1981 when he crashed his small airplane, leaving him temporarily with traumatic amnesia (unable to form new long-term memories), and he was forced to go on a sabbatical. He soon decided to return to Berkeley, under the pseudonym of Rocky Clark, in order to finish the computer science and electrical engineering courses needed to earn those degrees. Although he dropped out again, he eventually was given credit for his work at Apple, and the school awarded him a bachelor of science degree in electrical engineering in 1987.

Wozniak returned to Apple in 1982, though he resisted efforts to involve him in management. He finally retired as an active employee in 1985, immediately after being awarded, along with Jobs, a National Medal of Technology by President Ronald W. Reagan. Wozniak spent the ensuing decades engaged in philanthropic causes, especially involving the education of children, and in volunteer work teaching computer enrichment classes to preteens.

Although Wozniak was semiretired after leaving Apple, he kept up with the computing world by funding various business ventures and occasionally serving as an adviser or board member for different companies. In 2009 he became the chief scientist at Fusion-Io, an American company that produces high-capacity, solid-state storage devices. Wozniak was serving on the company's board of directors when he decided to become a full-time employee.

In 2006 Wozniak published his autobiography, *iWoz: Computer Geek to Cult Icon: How I Invented the Personal Computer, Co-Founded Apple, and Had Fun Doing It*.

TIM BERNERS-LEE

(b. June 8, 1955, London, Eng.)

English computer scientist Tim Berners-Lee is generally credited as the inventor of the World Wide Web. In 2004 he was awarded a knighthood by Queen Elizabeth II of the United Kingdom and the inaugural Millennium Technology Prize (€1 million) by the Finnish Technology Award Foundation.

Computing came naturally to Berners-Lee, as both of his parents worked on the Ferranti Mark I, the first commercial computer. After graduating in 1976 from the University of Oxford, Berners-Lee designed computer software for two years at Plessey Telecommunications, Ltd., located in Poole, Dorset, England. Following this, he had several positions in the computer industry, including a stint from June to December 1980 as a software engineering consultant at CERN, the European particle physics laboratory in Geneva.

While at CERN, Berners-Lee developed a program for himself, called Enquire, that could store information in files that contained connections ("links") both within and among separate files—a technique that became known as hypertext. After leaving CERN, Berners-Lee worked for Image Computer Systems, Ltd., located in Ferndown, Dorset, where he designed a variety of computer systems. In 1984 he returned to CERN to work on the design of the laboratory's computer network, developing procedures that allowed diverse computers to communicate with one another and researchers to control remote machines. In 1989 Berners-Lee drew up a proposal for creating a global hypertext document system that would make use of the internet. His goal was to provide researchers with the ability to share their results, techniques, and practices

Tim Berners-Lee (b. 1955) is the inventor of the World Wide Web.

without having to exchange email constantly. Instead, researchers would place such information "online," where their peers could immediately retrieve it anytime, day or night. Berners-Lee wrote the software for the first web server (the central repository for the files to be shared) and the first web client, or "browser" (the program to access and display files retrieved from the server), between October 1990 and the summer of 1991. The first "killer application" of the Web at CERN was the laboratory's telephone directory—a mundane beginning for one of the technological wonders of the computer age.

From 1991 to 1993 Berners-Lee evangelized the web. In 1994 in the United States he established the World Wide Web (W3) Consortium at the Massachusetts Institute of Technology's Laboratory for Computer Science. The consortium, in consultation with others, lends oversight to the Web and the development of standards. In 1999 Berners-Lee became the first holder of the 3Com Founders chair at the Laboratory for Computer Science. His numerous other honors include the National Academy of Engineering's prestigious Charles Stark Draper Prize (2007). Berners-Lee is the author, along with Mark Fischetti, of *Weaving the Web: The Original Design and Ultimate Destiny of the World Wide Web* (2000).

BILL GATES

(b. Oct. 28, 1955, Seattle, Wash., U.S.)

American computer programmer and entrepreneur William Henry Gates III cofounded Microsoft Corporation, the world's largest personal-computer software company.

Gates wrote his first software program at the age of 13. In high school he helped form a group of programmers who computerized their school's payroll system and founded Traf-O-Data, a company that sold traffic-counting systems to local governments. In 1975 Gates, then a sophomore at Harvard University, joined his hometown friend Paul G. Allen to develop software for the first microcomputers. They began by adapting BASIC, a popular programming language used on large computers, for use on microcomputers. With the success of this project, Gates left Harvard during his junior year and, with Allen, formed Microsoft. Gates's sway over the infant microcomputer industry greatly increased when Microsoft licensed an operating system called MS-DOS to International Business Machines Corporation—then the world's biggest computer supplier and industry pacesetter—for use on its first microcomputer, the IBM PC (personal computer). After the machine's release in 1981, IBM quickly set the technical standard for the PC industry, and MS-DOS likewise pushed out competing operating systems. While Microsoft's independence strained relations with IBM, Gates deftly manipulated the larger company so that it became permanently dependent on him for crucial software. Makers of IBM-compatible PCs, or clones, also turned to Microsoft for their basic software. By the start of the 1990s he had become the PC industry's ultimate kingmaker.

Largely on the strength of Microsoft's success, Gates amassed a huge paper fortune as the company's largest individual shareholder. He became a paper billionaire in 1986, and within a decade his net worth had reached into the tens of billions of dollars—making him by some estimates the world's richest private individual. With few interests beyond software and the potential of information technology, Gates at first preferred to stay out of the public eye, handling civic and philanthropic affairs indirectly through one of his foundations. Nevertheless, as Microsoft's power and reputation grew, and especially as it attracted the attention of the U.S. Justice Department's antitrust division, Gates, with some reluctance, became a more public figure. Rivals (particularly in competing companies in Silicon Valley) portrayed him as driven, duplicitous, and determined to profit from virtually every electronic transaction in the world. His supporters, on the other hand, celebrated his uncanny business acumen, his flexibility, and his boundless appetite for finding new ways to make computers and electronics more useful through software.

All of these qualities were evident in Gates's nimble response to the sudden public interest in the internet. Beginning in 1995 and 1996, Gates feverishly refocused Microsoft on the development of consumer and enterprise software solutions for the internet, developed the Windows CE operating system platform for networking noncomputer devices such as home televisions and personal digital assistants, created the Microsoft Network to compete with America Online and other internet providers, and, through Gates's company Corbis, acquired the huge Bettmann photo archives and other collections for use in electronic distribution.

In addition to his work at Microsoft, Gates was also known for his charitable work. With his wife, Melinda, he launched the William H. Gates Foundation (renamed the Bill & Melinda Gates Foundation in 1999) in 1994 to fund global health programs as well as projects in the Pacific Northwest. During the latter part of the 1990s, the couple also funded North American libraries through the Gates Library Foundation (renamed Gates Learning Foundation in 1999) and raised money for minority study grants through the Gates Millennium Scholars program. In June 2006 Warren Buffett announced an ongoing gift to the foundation, which would allow its assets to total roughly $60 billion in the next 20 years. At the beginning of the 21st century, the foundation continued to focus on global health and global development, as well as community and education causes in the United States. After a short transition period, Gates relinquished day-to-day oversight of Microsoft in June 2008—although he remained chairman of the board—in order to devote more time to the Bill & Melinda Gates Foundation.

It remains to be seen whether Gates's extraordinary success will guarantee him a lasting place in the pantheon of great Americans. At the very least, historians seem likely to view him as a business figure as important to computers as John D. Rockefeller was to oil. Gates himself displayed an acute awareness of the perils of prosperity in his 1995 best seller, *The Road Ahead*, where he observed, "Success is a lousy teacher. It seduces smart people into thinking they can't lose."

LINUS TORVALDS

(b. Dec. 28, 1969, Helsinki, Fin.)

Finnish computer scientist Linus Torvalds was the principal force behind the development of the Linux operating system.

At age 10 Torvalds began to dabble in computer programming on his grandfather's Commodore VIC-20. In 1991, while a computer science student at the University of Helsinki (M.S., 1996), he purchased his first personal computer (PC). He was not satisfied, however, with the computer's operating system (OS). His PC used MS-DOS (the disk operating system from Microsoft Corp.), but Torvalds preferred the UNIX operating system he had used on the university's computers. He decided to create his own PC-based version of UNIX. Months of determined programming work yielded the beginnings of an operating system known as Linux. In 1991 he posted a message on the internet to alert other PC users to his new system, made the software available for free downloading, and, as was a common practice among software developers at the time, he released the source code, which meant that anyone with knowledge of computer programming could modify Linux to suit their own purposes. Because of their access to the source code, many programmers helped Torvalds retool and refine the software, and by 1994 Linux kernel (original code) version 1.0 was released.

Operating Linux required a certain amount of technical acumen; it was not as easy to use as more popular operating systems such as Windows, Apple's Mac OS, or IBM OS/2. However, Linux evolved into a remarkably reliable, efficient system that rarely crashed. Linux became popular in the late 1990s when competitors of Microsoft began taking the upstart OS seriously. Netscape Communications Corp., Corel Corp., Oracle Corp., Intel Corp., and other companies announced plans to support Linux as an inexpensive alternative to Windows. In addition to Linux being free, its source code can be viewed and freely modified by anyone, unlike a proprietary OS. This means that different language versions can be developed and deployed in markets that would be too small for the traditional companies. Also, many organizations and governments have expressed security reservations about using any kind of computer software that contains code that cannot be viewed. For all of the above reasons, localized versions of Linux have become common in China and in many other non-Western countries.

In 1997 Torvalds took a position with Transmeta Corp., a microprocessor manufacturer, and relocated to California. Six years later he left the company to work as a project coordinator under the auspices of the Open Source Development Labs (OSDL), a consortium created by such high-tech companies as IBM, Intel, and Siemens to promote Linux development. In 2007 OSDL merged with the Free Standards Group to form the Linux Foundation.

SERGEY BRIN AND LARRY PAGE

respectively, (b. Aug. 21, 1973, Moscow, U.S.S.R. [now Russia]); (b. March 26, 1973, East Lansing, Mich., U.S.)

On August 19, 2004, Sergey Brin and Larry Page went from being promising computer science graduate students to multibillionaire technology mavens when Google, Inc., the online search engine company they had founded in 1998, issued its much-anticipated initial public offering (IPO). By creating the easy-to-use hypertext search engine Google, one of the most successful applications in the history of the internet, Brin and Page had provided World Wide Web browsing at its simplest to millions of ordinary computer users and had added a new verb, *to google*, to the English language.

Sergey Brin

Sergey Brin's family moved from Moscow to the United States in 1979. After receiving degrees (1993) in computer science and mathematics at the University of Maryland, he entered Stanford University's graduate program, where he met Page, a fellow graduate student. The two were both intrigued by the idea of enhancing the ability to extract meaning from the mass of data accumulating on the internet, and together they began working to devise a new type of search technology that leveraged web users' own ranking abilities by tracking each site's "backing links"—that is, the number of other pages linked to them. Brin received his master's degree in 1995, but he went on leave from Stanford's doctorate program to continue working on the search engine.

In mid-1998 Brin and Page began receiving outside financing, and they ultimately raised about $1 million from investors and from family and friends. They called their updated search engine Google—a name derived from a misspelling of the originally planned name, googol (a mathematical term for the number 1 followed by 100 zeros)—and created the corporation Google, Inc. Brin became the company's president of technology, and by mid-1999, when Google received $25 million of venture capital funding, the search engine was processing 500,000 queries per day. Google then became the client search engine for Yahoo!, one of the web's most popular sites, and by 2004 users were accessing the website 200 million times a day (roughly 138,000 queries per minute). On August 19, 2004, Google, Inc., issued its IPO, which netted more than $3.8 billion dollars for Brin.

In 2006 Google acquired YouTube, the web's most popular site for user-submitted streaming video, for $1.65 billion in stock. The move reflected the company's efforts to expand its services beyond internet searches. That same year Google was criticized for agreeing to comply with the Chinese government's censorship requirements—blocking websites extolling democracy, for example, or those covering the 1989 demonstrations in Tiananmen Square. Brin defended the decision, saying that Google's ability to supply some, albeit restricted, information was better than supplying none.

Larry Page

Lawrence Edward Page, whose father was a professor of computer science at Michigan State University, received a computer engineering degree from the University of Michigan (1995) and entered into the doctorate program at Stanford, where he met Brin. Working from Page's dormitory room, they began to devise their revolutionary search engine technology, which they initially dubbed BackRub. Most search engines simply returned a list of websites ranked by how often a search phrase appeared on them. Brin and Page incorporated into the search function the number of links each website had—i.e., a website with thousands of links would logically be more valuable than one with just a few links, and the search engine thus would place the heavily linked site higher on a list of possibilities. Further, a link from a heavily linked website would be a more valuable "vote" than one from a more obscure website. Meanwhile, the partners established an idealistic 10-point corporate philosophy that included "Focus on the user and all else will follow," "Fast is better than slow," and "You can make money without doing evil." In 1990 the two founded Google, with Page the new company's president of products. Google, Inc.'s, IPO in 2004 netted Page more than $3.8 billion.

GLOSSARY

cathode: The source of electrons in an electrical device.

cystic fibrosis: A disease of the exocrine glands that affects the pancreas, respiratory system, and sweat glands when glands produce an abnormally viscous mucus.

emphysema: A chronic disease of the lungs in which the air sacs become stretched and enlarged, decreasing the capability to supply oxygen to the blood.

hydrolysis: The decomposition of a compound caused by its reaction with water.

microprocessor: An integrated computer circuit that contains a processor (CPU).

patent: Rights given to a person by the government to make, use, or sell an invention.

polymer: A chemical compound made of smaller, repeating molecules linked together.

prototype: An original model on which something is based.

transistor: An electronic device that can transform weak electrical signals into strong ones, acting as an amplifier.

For More Information

BOOKS

Cooke, Tim. *The Book of Inventions: Amazing Ideas That Changed the World.* London, UK: Welbeck Publishing Group, 2020.

Gifford, Clive. *100 Things to Know About Inventions.* Mission Viejo, CA: Happy Yak, 2021.

González, Echo Elise. *The Internet*. Chicago, IL: World Book, 2020.

Morkes, Andrew, and Shaina C. Indovino. *Women Inventors.* Hollywood, FL: Mason Crest, 2022.

WEBSITES

Biography: Steve Jobs
www.biography.com/business-leaders/steve-jobs
Read more about the life and inventions of this American pioneer.

Johns Hopkins Medicine: How Does an MRI Scan Work?
www.hopkinsmedicine.org/health/treatment-tests-and-therapies/magnetic-resonance-imaging-mri
This site offers a brief explanation of the technology behind and uses for an MRI scan.

National Museums Scotland: Dolly the Sheep
www.nms.ac.uk/explore-our-collections/stories/natural-sciences/dolly-the-sheep/
Learn more about Dolly, the world's first cloned mammal created from an adult cell.

Science History Institute: Stephanie L. Kwolek
www.sciencehistory.org/education/scientific-biographies/stephanie-l-kwolek/
You can find a biography of Stephanie Kwolek, complete with photos and videos, on this website.

Index